Cecil C. Kuhne III

The Little Book of BBQ Law

American Bar Association
Defending Liberty
Pursuing Justice

Cover design by Andrew Alcala/ABA Design.

Printed in the United States of America.

17 16 15 14 13 5 4 3 2 1

Library of Congress Cataloging-in-Publication Data on File

ISBN: 978-1-61438-945-3

Table of Contents

Introduction

Everyone has his or her favorite barbecue joint. Mine happens to be in Amarillo, Texas, in a 1940s shotgun shack that is maybe twelve feet wide and forty feet long. Seating is in old school desks, and the linoleum on the floor, yellow with age, has clearly never been changed. The guy behind the counter—who looks like he too is from the '40s—takes your order as he pulls out a sheet of butcher paper and then starts methodically chopping on the brisket behind him. His affable sister rings up the bill on an old adding machine that undoubtedly predates World War II. The cheap wood paneling contains the typical signs: "No shoes, no shirt, no service" and "Bus your own table." There is, however, one slight nod to modernism: "Vegans are welcome here, but your options are very limited."

However you spell it—barbecue, barbeque, bar-B-Q, or BBQ (among many other variations)—this delicious fare is clearly an American institution. Aside from its interesting etymology (the spelling variations, whether you are referring to the food, the outdoor event, or the grill itself), barbecue also has a serious legal side, and a significant amount of litigation has sprung forth from these smoky flames, presenting some very engaging judicial decisions.

* * *

First of all, the world of barbecue can be more dangerous than you might imagine, as witnessed by a number of fascinating opinions in the realm of personal injury law:

- John Fragala volunteered at a cookout for a little league baseball team. He was turning chickens on a large barbecue grill owned by the city when the lid fell on his right hand, fracturing the middle finger and causing serious ligament damage. The pressing question before the court was whether the city was liable for his injuries under either a strict liability or negligence theory.

- The owners of a concrete company decided to hold a dinner for its employees, and several of them were asked to dig a barbecue pit. After the job was finished, they drove to a nearby lake to "clean up." While there, Horace Musick was injured when he jumped off a diving board. The central issue was whether, at the time of the accident, he was within the scope of employment and therefore entitled to workers' compensation benefits.
- Sylvia Rolin entered the Wal-Mart store in Athens, Alabama, where she tripped and fell over a barbecue-grill display and broke her hip in the process. The court had to decide whether the company had allowed an unreasonably dangerous condition to exist and was therefore liable for her injuries.
- The McRoys purchased a barbecue grill that was serviced three times by Sears Repair Service, who, among other things, installed a new burner assembly manufactured by Modern Home Products (MHP). The McRoys ultimately had some trouble with their esteemed grill, and somehow it caught fire, spreading flames to the exterior of their home. The thorny dilemma was whether there was culpability on the part of Sears and MHP.
- While shopping at the grocery store, Virginia McCauley slipped on a piece of bread soaked in barbecue sauce. The challenge facing the court was whether the owner of the store failed to discover the hazard in a timely fashion and was therefore liable for Mrs. McCauley's injuries.
- A Safeway bread-making facility in Denver threw a barbecue for its employees, and the company decided to change out the twenty-pound propane tank for a forty-pound one. The tank exploded and injured two employees, prompting

the Occupational Safety and Health Administration to issue a citation. The court was faced with the decision of whether the company had a general duty to provide a safe workplace.

* * *

Barbecue is big business, so naturally you have plenty of litigation concerning its myriad commercial transactions:

- Louis Christen sold his barbecue accessory company, and as part of the sale, he signed a noncompetition agreement. About a year later, he started a consulting business that offered advice to many of his former company's competitors. The conundrum before the bench was whether a consultancy was prohibited since Christen had no direct ownership in any competing business.
- George Schafer, a barbecue sauce developer, sued his former business partner, John Spence, after Spence obtained Schafer's secret spice formula and attempted (without success) to duplicate the sauce. The interesting question was whether there was an actionable conversion of the highly guarded recipe.
- Pace Industries manufactures barbecue grill bodies, and it ships them to a leased warehouse in Columbus, Georgia, where they are briefly stored until they are needed by the Char-Broil company. The judge had to determine whether Pace was entitled to the state's freeport tax exemption, since 95 percent of its products are sent out of state once they are incorporated into finished grills.
- Maurice Bessinger and his Piggie Park Enterprises, Inc. operated a chain of successful barbecue restaurants in South Carolina that also sold its sauce to grocery stores, who

boycotted the products when the restaurants started flying the Confederate flag. The point of contention was whether the ban violated the South Carolina Unfair Trade Practices Act.

- Richard Hartung's barbecuing was responsible for a fire that destroyed his apartment in Mammoth Lakes, California. The novel question before the bench was whether his live-in girlfriend, who actually owned the grill, could also be held responsible for the damage under a joint venture theory.
- Marie Livingston worked as a waitress in her former husband's barbecue business without compensation, and after he sold the business, she went to work for another barbecue restaurant in the same city. The issue was whether she was bound by the noncompetition clause in the sale contract of her former husband's company.
- Holsum Foods bottled K.C. Masterpiece barbecue sauce with ingredients provided by the Kingsford Company. When glass shards were found in the bottles, Kingsford demanded that Holsum pay them over a million dollars in damages. Holsum did so and then made a claim against its liability insurance company, who refused to pay. The vexing dilemma for the court was whether a policy exclusion applied.
- After obtaining the requisite governmental permits, Arthur Fincher opened a barbecue stand in Union, South Carolina. Some of the residential neighbors began to complain of the noise and less-than-desirable characters that frequented the business, so the city council passed an ordinance that severely restricted its hours of operation. The judge was faced with the decision of whether the ordinance deprived Fincher of his property rights.

* * *

Trademarks and trade names are important in establishing barbecue brands, and the courts have dealt with some very interesting issues:

- Kraft Foods produces a popular line of barbecue sauce known as Bull's-Eye (with annual sales of over $45 million), and the company was apparently not too amused by the appearance of a rival brand called Raging Bull. The critical issue was whether there was sufficient evidence of trademark infringement to enjoin sales of the competitor.
- The owner of the popular Chicago barbecue joint called Smoke Daddy moved to protect its turf by bringing a trademark infringement suit to prevent competition nearby from using the similar name Bone Daddy. The challenging question facing the court was the amount of confusion that would occur in the minds of consumers.
- The venerable makers of Kingsford charcoal brought suit against a small company that made barbecue sauce that bore the name Kingsfords, Inc. and was owned by Stephen and Marianne Kingsford. The unresolved issue was whether the charcoal company's trademark extended to barbecue sauce and barbecuing in general.
- Hesmer Foods sold a trademarked product called Beanee Barbecue, which found it difficult to compete with the less expensive Barbecue Beans sold by Campbell Soup Company. The court considered allegations of trademark infringement and unfair competition.

* * *

And last, but certainly not least, is the tumultuous area of labor law:

- A Los Angeles Police Department investigation found officer Bryan Haney, who had attended a barbecue with three other colleagues while on duty, guilty of leaving his post without authorization and submitting a false report. The court was faced with the decision of whether to uphold the suspension.

* * *

My colleagues at work—especially around lunchtime—often engage in the vigorous age-old debate about which is the best barbecue joint. Most recently, one of them was adamantly extolling the virtues of a particular dive (really a trailer house) in Austin, Texas, four hours away. "This is not just the best *barbecue* in the world," he exclaimed. "It's the best *food* in the world."

I was there the next day.

The Little Book of BBQ Law

Part I

In Harm's Way

Chapter One

Beware the BBQ Pit:

Assessing Liability

Fragala v. City of Rayville, 557 So. 2d 1118 (La. 1990)

One fine summer day, John Fragala performed his civic duty by volunteering at a cookout held by the Moose Lodge in Rayville, Louisiana, to benefit a little league baseball team. The city owned two massive metal barbecue pits, which it lent to nonprofit groups in the area. And at this point, it should be noted that these were no *diminutive* grills—each was over eight feet long and was equipped with four heavy doors that lifted up and back until they came to rest against a metal stop.

In the course of cooking, Fragala raised one of the doors and placed his right hand into the grill to turn some of the chickens inside. At that very moment, the lid fell abruptly on his hand, fracturing the middle finger and causing severe ligament damage, which he claimed would permanently hinder him in the performance of his job.

Fragala filed a lawsuit for damages against the city of Rayville, alleging both strict liability and negligence. In essence, he alleged that (a) the accident was caused due to the defective design, construction, and maintenance of the barbecue pit, and (b) the city had prior knowledge of these issues and failed to take adequate steps to correct them.

A trial was held on the merits. Fragala attempted to prove that the design of the barbecue pit was defective in that the lids, once opened, were unstable and could easily fall, thereby causing injury. He also sought to show that the city of Rayville was aware of this dangerous propensity by presenting a witness who saw one of the lids drop on his uncle several years earlier. Fragala also questioned the mayor of Rayville about an incident in which the mayor himself was cooking on one of the city's barbecue pits when the lid fell shut and injured his head.

To scientifically bolster his case, Fragala presented the testimony of an expert in mechanical engineering to establish that the barbecue pit possessed a defect in design or construction. This expert testified that the lids of the barbecue pits weighed approximately forty-five pounds each, excluding trim, handles, and smoke stacks. He stated that the opened lids were designed to rest against metal stops but did so only a few degrees beyond the point at which the lid was balanced vertically on its hinge. According to the expert, this was a very unstable position, and only a small amount of pressure would cause the lid to close. The expert concluded that the lids on the barbecue pits, as they existed at the time of the accident, were unreasonably dangerous.

Fragala then offered evidence to show that the city of Rayville had actual or constructive notice of this defect in the barbecue pits. To do so, he called the mayor of Rayville, who stated that some eight years ago the lid of one of the barbecue pits did fall on his head. But on cross-examination he admitted that he did not lift the lid all the way back against the metal stop before releasing it, and therefore, the accident was caused by his own negligence and not by any defect in the barbecue pit. The mayor also testified that the barbecue pits had been owned by the city for a number of years and that no one else had complained about them.

Fragala then presented the testimony of Ronnie Sanford, an actual witness to the accident. Sanford related that six or seven years before the accident, he saw a lid on one of the barbecue pits close shut on his uncle. Curiously enough, this uncle was not called to the stand to testify, nor was it shown that he ever reported the accident to city officials.

At the close of the plaintiff's evidence, the city moved for involuntary dismissal. The trial court, agreeing that the plaintiff had failed to adequately establish his case, granted the defendant's motion. In the court's view, the fatal flaw in the plaintiff's case was the lack of showing notice by the city of a defect in the barbecue pit, along with the observation that the brief testimony of a few prior accidents was inadequate to do so. The plaintiff appealed, but in the end, the appellate court ruled that the trial court had properly acted within its discretion.

The message of the court to Mr. Fragala was crystal clear—the next time you decide to barbecue chicken for the little league, you might want to consider wearing one of their baseball mitts.

Cue Spot 1

Old-Fashioned Texas Brisket

Ingredients

- 5 to 6 pounds of brisket (trimmed but left with a layer of fat about 1/4 inch thick)
- 6 cups hickory wood chips (soaked in water for about 30 minutes)
- 1 teaspoon black pepper
- 1 teaspoon brown sugar
- 1 teaspoon cayenne pepper
- 3 tablespoons chili powder
- 1 teaspoon cumin
- 1 tablespoon garlic powder
- 1 tablespoon onion powder
- 1 teaspoon oregano
- 2 tablespoons paprika
- 2 tablespoons salt

Preparation Instructions

1. Rinse brisket thoroughly and pat dry. In a small bowl, stir together spices, and rub brisket with spice mixture on all sides.
2. Place soaked chips into tin foil placed directly on coals. Place brisket fat side up in a large disposable aluminum pan in the center of the grate.

3. Slowly grill brisket at about 200°F for about 6 to 8 hours until tender. Add coals and wood chips as necessary to maintain constant temperature.
4. Transfer brisket to cutting board to cool. Slice across the grain.

Yield: 4 servings

Chapter Two

Workers' Compensation:

The Scope of Employment

Fidelity & Casualty Co. of New York v. Musick, 562 S.W.2d 38 (Tex. Civ. App.—Tyler 1978)

Here the legal issue before the court was a relatively straightforward one: Where does the job end and the fun begin?

Horace Musick was employed as a truck driver for Permanent Concrete Company, and the current job site was near the town of Greenville, Texas. The foreman, Floyd Johnson, suggested an outdoor barbecue as an incentive and as a reward for the hard work and dedication of the crew. He asked Musick for permission to host the outdoor fete on his land, and it was agreed that the event would be held Saturday evening. There still remained the job of digging a barbecue pit at the party site, so Musick and several other employees enthusiastically did so on the afternoon of the party.

After completing the pit, Musick and the others decided to go to a nearby lake to "clean up." Musick drove his personal truck to the lake, and while there, he seriously injured himself when diving into the water.

In his claim against the company for workers' compensation, Musick argued that "cleaning up," swimming, and diving into the lake were activities that could reasonably be expected to occur at such a company gathering, and therefore, they were within the course of employment. The jury found that Musick was totally and permanently disabled, and that because he was "at work," he was entitled to workers' compensation benefits.

On appeal, the extent and duration of Musick's disability were not disputed by the defendant, but five points of error were raised, all of which concerned whether Musick was acting within the course and scope of his employment.

The court observed that the normal deviation cases did not precisely apply here. This was a social outing, and an employee could arguably be held to have not left the service of his employer while participating at an event that was related to his employment. However, when an employee leaves the social event, goes to another site, and engages in a dangerous activity, such as the case here, the court felt the employee had clearly deviated and was no longer acting in the course of his job.

In the court's opinion, no evidence had been produced by Musick to show that the injury he suffered was actually related to his employment. The testimony reflected that no representative of Permanent Concrete ever directed Musick to go onto his neighbor's land and that the lake was sufficiently far enough away from Musick's land that he had to drive his own pickup truck to get there.

The fact that the injury was suffered away from the location of the party was, in the court's opinion, determinative. The court therefore held that, as a matter of law, the act of diving into the neighbor's pond was *not* an activity within the orbit of the corporate gathering in question.

The judgment of the trial court was reversed and rendered for the company. And Mr. Musick learned the hard way that going for a swim can rarely, if ever, be considered "working."

Cue Spot 2

Irresistible St. Louis Pork Ribs

Ingredients

- 3 to 4 pounds of spare ribs

For Rub

- 1 tablespoon black pepper
- 1/4 teaspoon cayenne pepper
- 1 tablespoon chili powder
- 1 tablespoon onion salt
- 1/4 cup brown sugar
- 1/4 cup sugar

For Sauce

- 1 1/2 teaspoons black pepper
- 1/4 teaspoon cayenne pepper
- 1 tablespoon chili powder
- 1/2 teaspoon ginger
- 2 cups ketchup
- 2 tablespoons honey
- 1 tablespoon mustard powder
- 1 tablespoon onion powder
- 1/3 cup brown sugar
- 1/4 cup apple cider vinegar
- 2 tablespoons Worcestershire sauce

Cue Spot 2 (continued)

Preparation Instructions

1. Trim spare ribs, removing excess fat. Rinse ribs and season with rub, and then cover and refrigerate for 4 hours or more.
2. Combine sauce ingredients in large pot. Bring to boil over high heat, stirring frequently to prevent sticking. Reduce temperature to low and simmer for at least 30 minutes.
3. Slowly grill ribs at about 200°F for about 5 or 6 hours, until tender.
4. Mop and baste ribs only during the last 30 minutes to prevent sauce from burning.

Yield: 4 servings

Chapter Three

Premises Liability: What Constitutes a Hazard?

Wal-Mart Stores v. Rolin, 813 So. 2d 861 (Ala. 2001)

Who would have thought that a routine trip to Wal-Mart could be so dangerous? Sylvia Rolin innocently entered the store in Athens, Alabama, one afternoon. While walking though a barbecue-grill display in the garden center, she tripped, fell, and broke her hip.

In due course, Rolin sued the corporate giant, alleging that it had negligently or wantonly caused or allowed an unreasonably dangerous condition to exist. The jury promptly agreed and returned a verdict in her favor for $150,000. Wal-Mart appealed on two grounds: (1) the trial court erred because the plaintiff had not proven that Wal-Mart had notice of the dangerous conditions alleged, and (2) the trial court erred in refusing to give the jury a curative instruction on comparative negligence requested by Wal-Mart.

Wal-Mart argued, first of all, that Rolin failed to show negligence because she never produced substantial evidence indicating that Wal-Mart breached its duty of care to her as an invitee. Wal-Mart maintained that, in fact, the evidence demonstrated that the company did not create a hazard, and that if a hazard existed, the company was not aware of it.

In the course of trial, Rolin testified that she and her husband Howard had entered the store, turned left, and stepped up onto the stepping-stones used in the barbecue-grill display. She claimed that she tripped over a grill in the aisle while walking on these stepping-stones and that she did not see it before she tripped. Mr. Rolin also testified that he and Mrs. Rolin walked on the six-foot-wide aisle of stepping-stones, and that when Mrs. Rolin fell, he noticed a barbecue grill sticking out of a box.

Pamela Whitman, an assistant manager at the store, testified that she was within ten feet of Rolin when she fell and that she did not see any merchandise sticking out from the display into the main aisle. She also said that there was *not* a six-foot-wide aisle of stepping-stones in the grill display as Rolin alleged.

Wal-Mart maintained that it therefore made a *prima facie* case, because it had no actual or constructive notice that a barbecue grill was sticking out of the box or that the grill display was hazardous. Rolin, however, argued that Wal-Mart created a dangerous condition when it constructed the barbecue-grill display.

After considering the issue of notice, the court held that when the defendant or its employees have affirmatively created a dangerous condition, the plaintiff need not introduce evidence that the defendant had actual or constructive knowledge of the hazard. Under such circumstances, the courts presume notice. In slip-and-fall cases involving a slippery substance of unknown origin, a plaintiff not only must make a showing that the fall was caused by a defect (the slippery substance) but must also present evidence that the defendant had, or should have had, notice of the defect at the time of the accident. But in a premises liability case, the question of whether the defendant had actual or constructive notice goes to the jury, regardless of whether the plaintiff has shown that the defendant had notice. In this case, the court said, there was evidence to indicate that the hazardous condition was created by employees of Wal-Mart, the premises owner.

Next, the court considered whether the trial court erred in failing to give a curative instruction in response to a question from the jury about comparative negligence, as Wal-Mart requested. For a better understanding of the issue presented, the following is the question and the judge's response:

> THE COURT: Thank you, ladies and gentlemen. I have a written question here, and let me just simply read this. I have discussed it with the attorneys. It says, **"If the plaintiff is guilty of one percent of guilt, do we rule for the defense?"**
>
> Let me answer it this way: I've gone through a charge of law for you, and I certainly can appreciate—I know these lawyers can appreciate that it's hard sometimes for you to digest all that, and I respect that. But, I can't go back and answer piecemeal questions without really going back through a pretty lengthy explanation of my charge again. Okay. **None of my charge had anything to do with percentages.**
>
> Let me simply say that. I don't mean to throw it back in your lap, but in essence, that's kind of where we are. It's just really not the type of question that I can just give an answer to. The only way I can answer this question—I've discussed this with the attorneys—is to really go back through a complete explanation of a lot of things, and if we get to that point, and we feel like that's necessary, certainly, we can do that. So I'm not being insensitive to your request, but I just don't think it's a question that I can answer at this point in time.
>
> I'm going to ask you all to please try to recollect as best you can everything that we dealt with here and the law that I charged you on and use that as a basis to try to work toward

> a verdict. Okay. Thank you very much. If you all would, you may go back to the jury room. (emphasis added)

Wal-Mart argued that the judge's use of the phrase "None of my charges had anything to do with percentages," in response to the jury's question, surely confused the jury as it contemplated the vexing issue of contributory negligence. The trial court's failure to give a curative instruction was, in Wal-Mart's estimation, a clearly reversible error. Not surprisingly, Rolin argued that the trial court properly charged the jury and did not err in refusing to give the requested instruction.

Regarding the jury charge, the appellate court pointed out that the question whether to grant a jury's request for additional instructions lay within the sound discretion of the trial court. The appellate court admitted that the better practice might have been to accede to such jury requests, but the court could not say that the failure to do so was a reversible error because it was not persuaded that the trial court's response was unduly weighted against Wal-Mart. The appellate court also noted that while the trial court did not reinstruct the jury on the law of contributory negligence, it did remind the jury to recall the entire charge as it had been given. In the court's mind, any error that might have resulted from the failure to give a curative instruction was a harmless one.

The trial court's judgment in favor of Mrs. Rolin was therefore affirmed, and in the process, the aisles of the Athens, Alabama, Wal-Mart were undoubtedly rendered a little safer for future barbecue shoppers.

Cue Spot 3

Magnificent Memphis Dry-Rub Ribs

Ingredients

- 3 to 4 pounds of spare ribs
- 1 teaspoon black pepper
- 1 teaspoon cumin
- 1 tablespoon brown sugar
- 1/2 teaspoon cayenne pepper
- 1/2 teaspoon celery seed
- 1 tablespoon dried onion flakes
- 1 teaspoon garlic powder
- 1/4 teaspoon oregano
- 1/2 teaspoon mustard powder
- 2 tablespoons paprika
- 1 teaspoon salt

Preparation Instructions

1. Wash ribs and pat dry. Combine ingredients in small bowl and stir. Rub 2/3 of this mixture on both sides of ribs.
2. Place ribs in a roasting pan and let marinate for at least 4 hours.

Cue Spot 3 (continued)

3. Slowly grill at about 200°F for about 5 or 6 hours until tender.
4. Sprinkle ribs with remaining rub.

Yield: 4 servings

Chapter Four

Grill on Fire:
Finding the Cause

Citizens Insurance Co. of America v. Sears Roebuck, 203 F. Supp. 2d 837 (W.D. Mich. 2002)

An exploding barbecue grill is nothing to be trifled with. Just ask Timothy and Linda McRoy.

They acquired the much-ballyhooed Model No. 8825, manufactured by Turco Manufacturing Company of Du Quoin, Illinois. The grill served them well for years, and during that period, it had been serviced three times by Sears Repair Service, who, among other things, had installed a new burner assembly manufactured by Modern Home Products (MHP). But the McRoys ultimately had some trouble with their beloved grill. Somehow it caught fire, and the flames spread quickly to the exterior of their home before the fire department was able to extinguish the blaze. In the end, the conflagration caused over $700,000 in damages to the home and its contents.

Acting as subrogee of the McRoys, Citizens Insurance Company filed suit against Sears and MHP, seeking recovery of the proceeds paid for losses incurred in the fire. The McRoys joined in the complaint as individual plaintiffs, seeking recovery for damages to real and personal property that exceeded the limits of the Citizens' policy, and incidental, consequential, and exemplary damages for embarrassment, fright, shock, humiliation, outrage, and indignity.

At trial, the service record of the grill was extensively examined. In addition to installing a new burner assembly, Sears technicians apparently had installed new cooking grids, lava rocks, and electrodes and cleaned the burner assembly. It was undisputed that after this thorough maintenance, the grill was fully operational. Furthermore, the McRoys could not identify any problems with the grill between the time it was last serviced and the fire.

The plaintiffs' complaint alleged that Sears entered into an agreement with the McRoys in which the company agreed to maintain and repair a number of appliances, including the Turco grill. It was undisputed that the grill functioned for more than three years after Sears replaced the burner assembly. In the court's mind, it could not be reasonably disputed that Sears fulfilled its contractual obligations to maintain the grill.

In their pleadings, the plaintiffs alleged that one of the burner's venture tubes became unintentionally disconnected. As the trial transpired, the evidence indicated how this could have occurred. During his deposition, one of the sons, Andrew McRoy, testified that shortly before the fire, he had "bumped into" the grill with a riding lawnmower while driving into the storage area. Andrew also indicated that as he and his brother prepared to use the grill, Andrew noticed that some internal components, including the cooking grate, some lava rocks, and a grate on which the lava rocks rested, had been displaced. Andrew admitted that this displacement could have occurred when he bumped into the grill with the lawnmower. He testified that he adjusted the grates and lava rocks, but he could not recall whether he moved the grill's burners.

Two days later, Fire Marshal Tom Spaman was dispatched to the McRoy's home to perform an investigation of the scene. Spaman was able to determine that the fire's point of origin was the grill and that the cause was accidental, but in his opinion, this did not necessarily mean the grill malfunctioned. Spaman could not determine whether any potential cause was more probable than not.

In its summary judgment motion, Sears argued that (a) it had no duty as a matter of law to equip the grill with post-market safety mechanisms, and (b) the plaintiffs could not establish that any conduct by Sears caused the fire. In its motion, MHP adopted the position of Sears and argued that the plaintiffs could not establish a breach of either product liability statute or warranty claim.

In the court's view, it made sense to first examine whether either Sears or MHP owed a duty to the plaintiffs, for if not, the remaining issues became moot. Under Michigan law, the supplier of a nondefective component part had no independent duty to analyze the design of the completed product. Here, the duties of a component part manufacturer were highly relevant because it was undisputed that neither MHP nor Sears designed, manufactured, or sold the original grill, and the plaintiffs themselves conceded that the grill, as originally manufactured, conformed with all industry safety standards.

As a supplier of replacement grill components, MHP clearly had a duty to ensure that its parts were reasonably safe for use as specified. The plaintiffs argued that MHP's replacement burner did not comply with applicable standards, which required burners to be secured against side-to-side or front-to-back displacement. However, assuming that movement of the burner assembly, which might occur when after being struck by a riding lawnmower, in fact caused the fire, the plaintiffs still faced the hurdle of establishing that the replacement burner would have failed the applicable safety standard.

The court also observed that the plaintiffs likewise failed to show that Sears was negligent in servicing the grill. This was not a situation in which the grill failed soon after being repaired. The grill performed well for over three years after replacement of the burner assembly and for approximately two and one-half years after the most recent service. There was simply no evidence, circumstantial or otherwise, indicating that Sears either breached its agreement with the McRoys or that it was negligent in its repair of the grill.

Even assuming that the plaintiffs could establish some breach of duty by either Sears or MHP, the plaintiffs still had to overcome the hurdle of establishing causation. The issue of causation, the court noted, was critical in this case. No one disputed that the fire originated in the grill. However, to withstand summary judgment, the plaintiffs had to establish that a genuine issue remained regarding their theory of how the fire started—in the burner—was more likely than not the cause of the fire.

The plaintiffs argued that their expert, Charles Krosp, located burn patterns on the grill's venture tubes, which indicated that these tubes were not in place at the time of the fire. However, Krosp's testimony did not address whether these patterns could have been produced by other causes, such as the impact of the burning ceiling as it fell on the grill. Even more important, however, was the fact that not one of the plaintiffs' experts—and there were many of them—was able to rule out other possible causes.

While no conclusive evidence established that either of the grill's venture tubes was dislodged at the time the fire started, it was possible that this had occurred when the grill was struck with the lawnmower. This evidence also permitted the inference that the impact of the lawnmower was sufficient to displace the grates, lava rocks, gas line, and regulator. This circumstantial evidence supported the inference that other elements of the grill, including the critical elements of the burner assembly, were likewise displaced. Without examination of these parts, other likely causes of the fire simply could not be excluded.

In the end, Sears and MHP were granted summary judgment, and the plaintiffs were ordered to take nothing. After the smoke cleared (so to speak), the court's ruling turned out to be judicial notice that gas grills generally don't work that well after they have been rammed by a riding lawnmower.

Cue Spot 4

Out-of-the-Park BBQ Chicken

Ingredients

- 4 large chicken breast halves (bone-in with skin)
- 1 clove garlic, minced
- 1 teaspoon butter
- 1/2 cup ketchup
- 1/4 cup brown sugar
- 1/4 cup chili powder
- 2 tablespoons Worcestershire sauce
- 1/2 tablespoon celery seed
- 1/2 teaspoon salt

Preparation Instructions

1. In a saucepan, sauté the garlic in butter until tender. Add remaining ingredients, and bring to a boil, stirring constantly. Remove from heat and set aside.
2. Grill chicken until almost done, turning occasionally.
3. Baste chicken with sauce, and grill for another 15 minutes.

Yield: 4 servings

Please
WATCH
YOUR
STEP

Chapter Five

Slip-and-Fall: Watching Your Step

McCauley v. Nicholas, 297 So. 2d 914 (La. 1974)

Virginia McCauley picked up her son Billy at Lee High School in Baton Rogue, Louisiana, and on their way home, they stopped briefly at the College Town Grocery. As Mrs. McCauley was leaving the store, she suddenly slipped and then fell forward from the top step. As a result, she suffered a severe fracture of her forearm. After she was taken to the hospital, it was discovered that there was a piece of bread soaked with barbecue sauce lodged on the sole of her shoe. Her son later recalled that although he did not see the bread, he did notice barbecue sauce on the side of her shoe immediately after the fall.

McCauley sued the owner of the premises, the Estate of Peter Materiste, and its lessee, Andrew Nicholas. The plaintiff predicated the liability of the Materiste Estate on the negligent design of the exit way and steps, and the liability of the lessee Nicholas on the failure to warn her of the hazardous condition. The jury rendered judgment in favor of the plaintiff for approximately $35,000, to be paid 85 percent by the Materiste Estate and 15 percent by Nicholas. From this adverse judgment, the defendants perfected this appeal.

The Materiste Estate assigned as error the lack of evidence to support the jury's finding of negligence concerning the design and construction of the steps. Nicholas claimed as error the jury's failure to find that he used reasonable care toward invitees. He contended that his inspections of the premises were reasonable and that the plaintiff offered no evidence to show that he had either actual or constructive knowledge of the foreign substance on which the plaintiff slipped.

It is black-letter law that a property owner owes to its invitees the duty of exercising reasonable care for their safety, and the owner is liable if the breach of that duty is the proximate cause of the accident. This duty includes exercising reasonable care to keep the premises in a safe condition and warning invitees about hidden perils of which the premises owner knows, or should know, in the exercise of reasonable care.

To prove his case, the plaintiff presented the testimony of Don Arnold, an architect who testified that the treads and risers of the steps were misshapen and not uniform, that there were no handrails or a landing for the plaintiff to step onto before descending the stairs, that the passageway was constricted, and that there were no signs warning invitees of these defects. However, Arnold admitted under cross-examination that anyone could safely traverse these steps with "minimal" attention and that all stairs pose some element of risk. The court also remarked that his evaluation was based upon national standards adopted by the state *after* the building was constructed.

The court concluded that McCauley did not slip because of any fault in the design or construction of the steps. In light of this and the fact that these steps could be traversed with minimal attention, the court found that the Materiste Estate was not liable for the plaintiff's injuries.

The court then assessed the liability of the lessee, Nicholas. It was clear that McCauley attributed the barbecue-soaked bread as the cause of her fall, as evidenced by this courtroom exchange:

Q: I believe you said you fell?

A: (Mrs. McCauley) Yes, sir.

Q: Okay. How did you fall?

A: I fell forward, bruising my arm and my knees.

Q: Do you recall where you fell, what part of the store you fell?

A: As I was coming out of the door, the first step.

Q: On the first step. Do you recall what you slipped on, what you fell on?

A: A piece of bread and it had barbecue sauce on it.

Q: All right. Now, you told us that you slipped on some kind of debris. What kind of debris do you think it was?

A: It was bread.

Q: But for that piece of bread you don't think you would have fallen?

A: I don't think I would have. The bread had barbecue sauce on it.

In regard to the liability of the lessee Nicholas, the court ruled that to avoid liability, the storekeeper must make a preliminary showing of a reasonably thorough inspection where there was a potential danger to patrons. While the burden was on the plaintiff to show that such substance remained on the floor longer than it should have been, this burden was subject to the requirement that the defendant first show that the foreign object was not discovered in spite of reasonably careful and frequent inspections.

In this regard, the court believed that Nicholas proved that he had made reasonable inspections of his premises under the circumstances. Nicholas testified that it was his daily routine to clean the steps in front of his store at 6:30 A.M. when he opened the store and again between the hours of 1:30 to 2:30 P.M. He also testified that he followed the same routine on the day of the accident, and his wife and his employee Marion Politz corroborated him in this.

The court was of the opinion that such inspections were reasonable under the particular situation of this case, as they coincided with the end of the lunch hour and after the peak of the defendant's "poor boy" sandwich business, at which time it would be more likely that such debris would be thrown about the premises. To require more would be to require that the defendant virtually become an insurer of his customers' safety, which the law did not require.

Having found that Nicholas, in spite of reasonable inspection procedures, failed to discover the extraneous substance on the front steps, the burden of proof was on the plaintiff to show how it got there or how it remained on the steps longer than it should have. The plaintiff offered no proof in either regard. The showing of reasonable inspections by the store owner and the failure of the plaintiff to produce any evidence to show either actual or constructive notice of the store owner rendered the jury's finding against the defendant Nicholas manifestly erroneous.

The plaintiff's suit was accordingly dismissed. And the next time Mrs. McCauley went to the grocery store to buy a loaf of bread, she was no doubt on the lookout for exemplars soaked in barbecue sauce.

Cue Spot 5

Classic Kansas City BBQ Sauce

Ingredients

- 2 cups ketchup
- 1/2 cup apple juice
- 1/2 cup apple cider vinegar
- 1/2 cup brown sugar
- 5 tablespoons butter
- 3 tablespoons paprika
- 2 tablespoons chili powder
- 4 garlic cloves, finely chopped
- 1/2 medium-sized onion, finely chopped
- 1/4 teaspoon salt
- 1/4 teaspoon cayenne pepper

Preparation Instructions

1. In a saucepan, sauté onion and garlic.
2. Add remaining ingredients and stir well. Simmer slowly for about 30 minutes.

Yield: about 4 cups

Chapter Six

Exploding Propane:
The Case for an OSHA Violation

Safeway v. Occupational Safety and Health Review Commission, 382 F.3d 1189 (10th Cir. 2004)

The venerable Safeway company operates a bread-baking facility in Denver, and periodically the company throws an outdoor barbecue for its employees. Safeway purchased a small gas grill equipped with a twenty-pound tank, but to ensure that it had sufficient fuel, the management substituted a more aggressive forty-pound tank. These larger tanks, however, have a warning label that clearly states that they should *not* be used with a grill supplied with a twenty-pound tank.

At one of these outdoor parties, the plant manager summoned the plant engineer and the day-shift maintenance foreman and informed them that the grill was not adequately cooking the meat. The two men attempted to improve the flow of gas by checking the regulator and by repositioning the tank. While they were doing so, fuel escaped and a massive ball of fire erupted. As a result, one of the men suffered severe burns to his hand, and the other had his facial hair singed.

After the accident, the Occupational Safety and Health Administration (OSHA) investigated the accident and issued a citation.

The citation alleged that Safeway had violated the general duty clause to provide its employees with a safe environment when it exposed them to "the release and ensuing fire of propane due to the improper use of a gas hose and regulator assembly in combination with a forty-pound cylinder." OSHA later amended the citation to include the alternative allegation that Safeway had specifically violated a regulation that required a compressed gas cylinder to be "properly supported to prevent it from being knocked over."

After a hearing, the administrative law judge (ALJ) affirmed the citation on the basis of the general duty clause. Safeway filed a petition for review in the Tenth Circuit Court of Appeals.

Safeway argued that it complied with all relevant regulations and that the Secretary of Labor had to demonstrate that there were no specific standards applicable to the cited condition before it could issue a citation under the general duty clause. But the court disagreed, pointing out that when the employer has knowledge of an obviously hazardous condition, compliance with specific standards does not relieve the employer of the responsibility under the general duty clause, which states:

> Each employer (1) shall furnish to each of his employees employment and a place of employment which are free from recognized hazards that are causing or are likely to cause death or serious physical harm to his employees; (2) shall comply with occupational safety and health standards promulgated under this chapter.

Therefore, the plain language of the statute and its structure indicates that an employer's duty to provide a safe working environment extended beyond compliance with specific safety standards that were included in regulations promulgated under the act.

The Tenth Circuit Court of Appeals pointed out that none of the regulations identified by the parties addressed one of the most obvious hazards: the use of a forty-pound tank with a grill designed for a twenty-pound tank. The ALJ concluded that the use of a forty-pound tank with an ordinary grill was a violation of the general duty clause. To show a violation of the general duty clause, the Secretary of Labor had to prove that (1) the employer failed to render its workplace free of an obvious and recognized hazard, (2) the hazard was causing or likely to cause death or serious physical harm, and (3) there was a feasible method by which the employer could have abated the hazard.

As the ALJ noted, the forty-pound tank itself included warnings against using it with a grill designed for twenty-pound tanks. In addition, the instructions supplied with the grill indicated that the propane tank should be installed underneath the frame of the grill so that the "bottom ring of the tank rests in notches in the tank support strap." Safeway supervisors were aware that the tank was too large to fit underneath the grill and that the tank could not be attached to the grill without a special adapter. Accordingly, there was substantial evidence to support the ALJ's finding that the use of the forty-pound tank was a hazard and that Safeway was keenly aware of it.

Likewise, there was substantial evidence supporting the ALJ's conclusion that using the forty-pound tank was likely to cause serious injury. The forty-pound tank was difficult to connect to the grill. Because of the size of the tank, it had to be tipped against the frame of the grill to allow connection to the grill. It was common knowledge that failing to properly secure a tank created a danger. Finally, it was clear that Safeway could have eliminated the hazard by simply using a twenty-pound tank.

Accordingly, the court affirmed the ALJ's decision, hopefully prompting the bakers at Safeway to read the grill instructions a little more closely the next time.

Cue Spot 6

Take-It-to-the-Bank BBQ Sauce

Ingredients

- 1 cup ketchup
- 1/2 cup water
- 1/4 cup onion, finely chopped
- 2 tablespoons garlic, minced
- 2 tablespoons butter
- 2 tablespoons molasses
- 2 tablespoons mustard
- 2 tablespoons brown sugar
- 1 tablespoon Worcestershire sauce
- 1 tablespoon paprika
- 1 tablespoon chili powder
- 2 teaspoons oregano
- 2 teaspoons thyme
- 1 teaspoon salt
- 1 teaspoon black pepper
- 1/4 teaspoon cayenne pepper

Preparation Instructions

1. In a saucepan, sauté onion and garlic. Add remaining ingredients, reduce heat, and simmer for about 30 minutes.

Yield: about 2 1/2 cups

Part II

This Business of BBQ

Chapter Seven

Noncompete Clause:

Strictly Construed

Jackes-Evans Manufacturing Co. v. Christen, 848 S.W.2d 553 (Mo. 1993)

Louis Christen owned a business that manufactured and sold barbecue accessories, but once the company became financially troubled, he reluctantly decided to liquidate it to pay back his creditors and avoid bankruptcy. As a result, Christen entered into negotiations to sell the company to Jackes-Evans Manufacturing Company.

Because Mr. Christen needed a paycheck and because Jackes-Evans had no experience in the barbecue business, Christen's employment by the company became a key part of the negotiations. Eventually, the parties executed a "Memorandum of Intent" summarizing the contemplated terms of employment in connection with the sale of assets. One of the terms was that Christen would agree "not to engage in any business in competition with the company for a period of five years after the termination of his employment."

The parties simultaneously executed a purchase agreement and an employment contract. Jackes-Evans agreed to pay Christen over a million dollars for certain assets, including inventory, tools, machinery, equipment, patents, and designs. In addition,

Jackes-Evans would employ Christen as the sales and marketing manager for a period of one year at a salary of $46,000 plus a commission on sales. The employment contract contained a thorough noncompetition agreement:

> Commencing on the first day of the time of this agreement and continuing for a period of five years, employee agrees that he will not, in any manner, directly or indirectly, **own, manage, operate, join, control, participate in or be connected as a partner, investor, advisor, consultant or otherwise** with any business or business entity which is involved in the manufacture and/or sale of home barbecue equipment in either the United States or Canada. (emphasis added)

Largely through the efforts of Christen, sales in the first year greatly exceeded Jackes-Evans's expectations. Christen was offered a new contract as marketing director with an annual salary of $60,000. However, because he was dissatisfied with the working conditions and because his ability to earn commissions was eliminated, Christen refused the position and terminated his employment at the end of the first year.

Christen immediately started his own business as a sole proprietor, offering consulting services in developing and marketing products. In the process, he contacted many of his former suppliers and customers, and in the first several months, he established business relationships with at least three competitors of Jackes-Evans. For example, Christen was paid $72,000 a year to act as an agent of a Taiwanese trading company that exported barbecue equipment to dealers in the United States. He also appeared at numerous trade shows and was instrumental in causing Jackes-Evans to lose its largest customer.

Predictably enough, Jackes-Evans filed suit to enforce the noncompetition agreement, and in court, Christen admitted that he was actively competing with the company. But he insisted that under the noncompetition agreement he was not prohibited from selling or acting as a representative as long as he did not "have an ownership interest" in a competing company. The trial court, interestingly enough, accepted this narrow interpretation of the contract and concluded that the noncompetition clause precluded *only* ownership or management activities, *not* mere employment. Accordingly, the trial court enjoined Christen from owning, managing, or acting as a marketing advisor and consultant to any barbecue accessory business but refused to enjoin him from acting as an *employee* for any such business.

The basis for this rather paradoxical order was the trial court's conclusion that the contract should be construed pursuant to the rule of *ejusdem generis*. This rule of construction, sometimes invoked as an aid in construing ambiguous documents where the intent of the parties is unclear, maintains that where general words follow particular ones, the general ones will be limited in their meaning to things of like kind with those particularly specified. Because all of the prohibited activities listed in the noncompetition clause related to ownership or management, the trial court held that the phrase "or otherwise" could not be construed to include employment.

The appellate court, however, roundly disagreed with that interpretation of the contract, and it noted that the principle of *ejusdem generis* had no application where the particular words described variant things or concepts. The court pointed out the prohibition against participating as a partner or investor was quite different from prohibiting a connection with a competitor as an advisor or consultant. The latter concept was certainly broad enough to include an employment relationship, and thus, it was error for the trial court to hold the phrase "or otherwise" to not apply to employment.

Moreover, the appellate court remarked that ascertainment of the intention of the parties in entering into the contract is the cardinal principle regarding judicial interpretation. To determine the intent of the parties, a court must consider the entire contract, its subsidiary agreements, the relationship of the parties, the subject matter of the contract, the facts and circumstances surrounding the execution of the contract, the practical construction the parties themselves have placed upon the contract by their acts and deeds, and all other external circumstances that cast light on the intent of the parties.

Accordingly, the appellate court felt that the evidence pointed unerringly to the conclusion that the parties intended to prohibit Christen from engaging in *any* competition, regardless of its form, in the barbecue equipment business. When it bought the business, Jackes-Evans was entering a new field of commerce in which it did not possess knowledge, experience, reputation, or contacts with suppliers and customers, and Christen was hired to supply these deficiencies. In the court's words, it would be "foolish" for Jackes-Evans to purchase Christen's services for one year and then permit him to destroy what he had brought to the company.

Whether Christen competed as an owner or as an employee would be of no import whatsoever as far as Jackes-Evans was concerned. Christen's agreement not to "engage" in any competing business for a five-year period was evidence that he was fully aware of and joined in this intent. After leaving his employment with Jackes-Evans, Christen warned some of the suppliers and customers not to tell Jackes-Evans about his dealings with them. Consideration of all these circumstances led to but a single conclusion regarding the intention of the parties: Christen agreed not to engage in competition with Jackes-Evans in *any* form or manner.

Accordingly, the appellate court issued a permanent junction enjoining Christen from competing with Jackes-Evans in the business of manufacturing or selling barbecue equipment for the period of five years.

And Mr. Christen thus learned the hard way that he could not sell his barbecue business and eat it too.

Cue Spot 7

Heart-of-Texas BBQ Sauce

Ingredients

- 1 1/2 cups ketchup
- 1/2 cup cider vinegar
- 1/2 cup white sugar
- 1/2 cup water
- 2 tablespoons Worcestershire sauce
- 1 tablespoon chili powder
- 1 teaspoon cumin
- 1/2 teaspoon cayenne pepper

Preparation Instructions

1. In a saucepan, stir together ingredients and bring to a low simmer for about 30 minutes.

Yield: about 3 cups

Chapter Eight

Secret Recipe:
A Question of Conversion

Schaefer v. Spence, 813 S.W.2d 92 (Mo. 1991)

As a restaurant cook at several dining establishments in Springfield, Missouri, George Schaefer began developing his barbecue sauce over a period of thirty years. As his unique sauce became increasingly popular, Schaefer sold it to customers of restaurants where he was employed and to a food wholesaler that distributed it to grocery stores throughout southwest Missouri.

Schaefer took great pains to maintain the secrecy of the critical ingredients in his recipe. Although he revealed the contents of the sauce base, he would not allow others, including fellow employees who helped him prepare it, to discover the identity and proportions of the various spices.

While Schaefer was employed at Tiny's Smokehouse, he met John Spence, and they discussed the possibility of having Spence market Schaefer's barbecue sauce. Schaefer gave Spence a price list and sauce samples, and the first day of sales was wildly successful—Spence obtained orders for twenty-four *cases*. Schaefer and Spence subsequently founded a company to produce and market Schaefer's sauce. Schaefer was a 50 percent shareholder in the newly formed corporation, Schaefer's Gourmet, Inc. and was responsible for production of the sauce. Spence was a fifty percent shareholder and was responsible for marketing and sales.

Schaefer arranged for Spicecraft, a St. Louis company that blended spices on a large scale for food companies, to prepare the voluminous amounts of the spice mixture that he anticipated Schaefer's Gourmet would need. Before he disclosed his formula to Spicecraft, a rather paranoid Schaefer obtained a nondisclosure letter from the company, and he demanded that all orders be sent to Schaefer at his residence.

Because of brisk demand for the sauce, Schaefer and Spence quickly realized the need to expand their production facilities, but they did not have the capital to do so. Schaefer objected to additional shareholders because he wanted to retain a 50 percent ownership in the company. He also balked at a bank loan, which would have required him to either make the sauce recipe a corporate asset or disclose it to the bank.

Schaefer and Spence, therefore, decided to abruptly end their business relationship, and they entered into an agreement in which Spence acquired Schaefer's shares and interest in the corporation and its assets. Schaefer also granted Spence a license for three years to bottle, market, and sell products under the trade name "Schaefer's Gourmet." The contract specifically provided that the barbecue sauce recipe would remain Schaefer's property, and it gave Spence a ninety-day option to acquire it for $50,000 plus a royalty on all sales during the two-year period following exercise of the option.

Spence could not afford to buy the recipe during the option period. Nevertheless, following a series of inquiries by letter, telephone, and personal visit he was able to somehow obtain from Spicecraft a copy of the formula and 1,000 pounds of the spice mixture. A prompt, and rather terse, letter from Schaefer's lawyer to Spence demanded that he cease using the recipe. The letter also advised: "It would appear that you owe Mr. Schaefer at least $50,000 for the recipe pursuant to the Purchase Agreement. In addition, it would appear that additional damages are recoverable for misappropriation and conversion of the recipe."

With the matter unresolved, Schaefer initiated this litigation. The suit went to trial on allegations of breach of contract, conversion, and fraud, and Schaefer sought actual damages of $50,000, plus punitive damages.

The trial court found that Spence intended to appropriate Schaefer's sauce but that his efforts met with failure. The court ruled that since Spence never succeeded in duplicating the barbecue sauce recipe, he never exercised dominion over Schaefer's property. Schaefer was therefore not entitled to damages under the allegation that Spence exercised the option but refused to pay the $50,000 fee. Schaeffer appealed the decision.

The appeal presented two basic questions: whether Spence's action in obtaining the spice blend formula constituted either (a) an exercise of the option or (b) conversion.

In point one, Schaefer argued that Spence exercised his option to buy the recipe by "wrongfully" acquiring the spice blend formula from Spicecraft. Schaeffer asserted that the degree of success in copying his sauce was irrelevant. The court, however, observed that acceptance of an option must generally be in accordance with the terms of the option and cannot be made in any other manner. The contract between Schaefer and Spence clearly specified the option was to be exercised by Spence's "written notification of his desire to purchase his recipe." The court ruled against Schaefer on this point.

In his second point, Schaefer contended the trial court erroneously denied him recovery on his conversion theory. In the court's view, this argument overlooked an important threshold inquiry: whether the spice blend formula was a species of property susceptible to conversion. The law of conversion, the court noted, is concerned with possession, not title. And while the idea that only tangible personal property could be converted had largely been discarded by the courts, conversion does *not* lie for the appropriation of an *idea*, and the present court felt it would be preferable to fashion other remedies, such as unfair competition, to protect such intangible assets from being misused.

At the news of the exculpatory decision, absconders of secret barbecue sauce recipes from around the country surely celebrated.

Cue Spot 8

Fabulous Eastern Carolina BBQ Sauce

Ingredients

- 1 cup white vinegar
- 1 cup cider vinegar
- 1 tablespoon brown sugar
- 1 tablespoon cayenne pepper
- 1 tablespoon hot pepper sauce
- 1 teaspoon salt
- 1 teaspoon black pepper

Preparation Instructions

1. Combine ingredients in a jar with a tight-fitting lid and mix well. Refrigerate for 1 to 2 days. Stir well before use.

Yield: about 2 1/2 cups

Chapter Nine

Grills in Transit:
Evading the Tax Man

Muscogee City Board of Tax Assessors v. Pace Industries, 705 S.E.2d 678 (Ga. 2010)

The taxing authorities usually win, and in this case, they were attempting to get their hot little hands on a peripatetic lot of barbecue grill parts.

Pace Industries manufactures die-cast aluminum bodies for gas and charcoal barbecue grills, which it transports from its Arkansas plant to a warehouse it leases in Columbus, Georgia, where they are stored until needed by Char-Broil, a major producer and distributor of barbecue grills. Char-Broil incorporates the grill bodies into the finished product, which Char-Broil then ships to its customers, mainly large retail stores. Char-Broil sends approximately 95 percent of its grills to customers *outside* the state of Georgia.

Pace applied to the Muscogee County Board of Tax Assessors for the freeport exemption for the inventory stored in its Columbus warehouse. The exemption applied generally to "inventory of finished goods held for shipment outside the state." To qualify for the statutory exemption, the inventory in question had to be (1) finished goods, (2) in Georgia for less than twelve months, and (3) destined for shipment to a final destination outside Georgia. Pace classified the grill bodies as finished goods for inventory accounting purposes on its books and records, and the tax board conceded that point. The board also agreed that Pace stored the grill bodies in Georgia for less than the twelve-month statutory maximum (the average inventory turnover rate was about fifty days). The board contended, however, that the grill bodies did *not* meet the third test, and thus, the issue was whether the grill bodies were "destined for shipment to a final destination outside this state."

After the board denied the exemption, Pace appealed to the Superior Court of Muscogee County. The trial court concluded that Pace's inventory of grill bodies did, in fact, qualify for the freeport exemption because they were destined for shipment to a final destination outside the state. The tax board then appealed this order.

In its argument before the appellate court, Pace contended that the grill bodies were destined for shipment to a final destination outside the state because Char-Broil promptly sold them to customers outside of Georgia. Pace concluded that nothing in the statute made it relevant that the grill bodies were first sent to Char-Broil before being shipped outside the state.

However, the appellate court ultimately disagreed, because as far as Pace was concerned, the final destination of the grill bodies *was* Char-Broil's plant in Georgia. The court pointed out that Pace did not merely send the grill bodies to Char-Broil—it *sold* them to Char-Broil. Unless exempted, Georgia law imposed *ad valorem* tax on all personal property. The tangible personal property exemption known as the freeport exemption was available for certain business inventory, but what became of the inventory in the hands of a purchaser was *not* relevant to the exemption. The court noted that in determining whether a retail sale was made, the court had to look to the location and conduct of the seller, rather than the location of the ultimate purchaser. As far as Pace was concerned, the "final destination" of the grill bodies was Char-Broil's Columbus plant.

Unfortunately, future purchasers of Char-Broil grills would inevitably see an increase in prices, as the company compensated for the aggressiveness of the Georgia tax collectors.

Cue Spot 9

Tantalizing Western Carolina BBQ Sauce

Ingredients

- 1 1/2 cups cider vinegar
- 1/2 cup brown sugar
- 1/2 cup ketchup
- 1/4 cup butter
- 2 tablespoons hot pepper sauce
- 2 tablespoons Worcestershire sauce
- 2 teaspoons mustard powder
- 1 teaspoon salt
- 1 teaspoon black pepper

Preparation Instructions

1. Mix ingredients in a saucepan and simmer about 30 minutes, stirring occasionally.
2. Place in covered container and refrigerate for 1 to 2 days. Stir well before use.

Yield: about 2 1/2 cups

Chapter Ten

Restaurant Boycott: An Unfair Practice?

Bessinger v. Bi-Lo, Inc., 622 S.E.2d 564 (S.C. 2005)

In the Deep South, the memory of the Confederacy dies hard for some.

Maurice Bessinger is a native South Carolina businessman and an officer and principal shareholder in Piggie Park Enterprises, whose burgeoning enterprise encompasses eleven restaurants and a sprawling plant for mass production of barbecue sauce that was sold in supermarkets.

In July 2000, after much controversy, the Confederate battle flag was at last removed from the statehouse dome. To compensate for what Bessinger saw as an injustice, he began flying a Confederate flag at each of his restaurants and distributing political literature. Numerous newspaper articles and broadcast media pieces criticized him for doing so, and as a result, several retail grocers promptly discontinued selling his products and removed the remaining stock from their shelves.

Bessinger sued nine corporate entities and several individual store managers, alleging that discontinuation of his products constituted violations of the South Carolina Unfair Trade Practices

Act (SCUTPA). After hearing the arguments of the parties, the trial judge issued an order dismissing the case. The court disagreed that the plaintiff had sufficiently pled the elements of an "unfair" act constituting an actionable grievance under SCUTPA, which declares unlawful "unfair acts or practices in the conduct of any trade or commerce." Under the vaguely worded statute, an act is unfair when it is "offensive to public policy" or when it is "immoral, unethical, or oppressive."

The appellate court agreed with the trial court that the allegations in the complaint did not show that the defendants committed acts that would be considered unfair under SCUTPA. Assuming (without deciding) that the defendants terminated their business relationships with the plaintiff solely because of Bessinger's actions or statements, the court concluded that there was no first amendment violation. Moreover, the court explained that as free market participants, the defendant grocery store chains and their respective managers had the right to choose with whom they conducted their business.

Although this right was not an "absolute, unfettered privilege," recent case law indicated that in South Carolina the enactment of SCUTPA had not affected this freedom. According to the court, the business decision to discontinue the sale of such items was best left to the one who bore the financial risk of that decision. It followed, then, that the courts should not mandate that a private enterprise maintain an association with an individual or organization that it believed—for whatever reason—was not conducive to any part of its business, including its marketing, public image, and organizational structure.

In other words, in South Carolina you have the right to fly the Confederate flag, but you also have the right *not* to do business with those who have the right to fly the Confederate flag.

Cue Spot 10

Decidedly Different Alabama BBQ Sauce

Ingredients

- 1 cup mayonnaise
- 1/2 cup apple cider vinegar
- 2 tablespoons lemon juice
- 2 tablespoons black pepper
- 1/2 teaspoon salt
- 1/2 teaspoon cayenne pepper

Preparation Instructions

1. Combine ingredients in bowl and stir.
2. Refrigerate for at least 8 hours before using. Brush over chicken, turkey, or pork during last few minutes of grilling.

Yield: about 2 cups

Chapter Eleven

Who's at Fault?: Imputing Negligence

Planck v. Hartung, 98 Cal. App. 3d 838 (1979)

An out-of-control barbecue-grill fire can do some serious damage. One such fire caused considerable destruction of the La Vista Blanc Condominiums in Mammoth Lakes, California. According to Jessie Planck, the owner of the condominium in question, the damage was caused by the lessee Richard Hartung, who was using a barbecue grill owned by the defendant Rita McDavid.

Hartung and McDavid were living together in the condominium but were not married. McDavid and her minor children had moved into Hartung's unit about six weeks before the fire and cohabitated with him as a family. McDavid had brought to the residence certain personal property, including the barbecue grill in question. It was an ordinary, kettle-type, charcoal-burning model with vents on the top and bottom, and it was used on an outdoor balcony.

Throughout the six-week period the barbecue was used some fifteen times, each time by Hartung alone and never by McDavid. On the date of the fire, Hartung prepared the coals, cooked the meat, and closed the hood. McDavid had absolutely nothing to do with regard to the barbecue. She was, however, the first to notice the fire after dinner that evening. Before that time, she was never aware of any danger related to the use of the barbecue or with the manner in which Hartung operated it.

Planck filed suit against McDavid, no doubt looking for access to another homeowner's insurance policy. McDavid responded with a motion for summary judgment based on the proposition that she did nothing—whether negligent, willful, or otherwise—to cause the fire and that she should therefore not be held accountable for the acts of Hartung. The trial court instantly agreed.

Planck persisted with various novel legal theories for the existence of triable issues against McDavid. She argued, first of all, that any negligence of Hartung must be imputed to McDavid because the two were engaged in a "joint venture." But the court found nothing to suggest any business purpose, profit motive, or tangible benefit to Hartung and McDavid from their living arrangement, other than that which is typical in all families. McDavid had made no oral or written agreement to assume liability for any acts or omissions of Hartung. The facts that McDavid usually cooked the meals, that Hartung gave her money for groceries, that they combined kitchen utensils, and that McDavid did the shopping did not, in the court's mind, change this relationship into a joint venture for vicarious or imputed liability purposes.

As the court tersely concluded: "If Hartung and McDavid had been married, there would have been no liability on the part of McDavid. *A fortiori* there is none here."

Not about to relent, the plaintiff then contended that there was a triable issue of fact regarding McDavid's own asserted negligence—McDavid was in "actual possession" of the unit; she owned the barbecue, she permitted Hartung to operate it, she failed to instruct Hartung in its use, she neglected to inspect it while living there, and she "quite possibly" was on the balcony on the evening of the alleged accident.

The court once again did not agree. In its view, neither individually nor collectively did these facts show negligence. There was no negligence in McDavid's failure to inspect or instruct on the use of a simple barbecue grill. Hartung had used the item without incident at least fifteen times before the fire, obviously inspecting it each time. There was really nothing to check anyway but the vent, and inspection by McDavid would have revealed no more than what Hartung had seen.

After all was said and done, the court ultimately concluded that the culpability of a barbecue grill fire lies not with its owner but with the chef who lit it.

Cue Spot 11

Off-the-Charts Steak Marinade

Ingredients

- 1/2 cup olive oil
- 1/4 cup balsamic vinegar
- 1/4 cup soy sauce
- 2 teaspoons garlic, minced
- 1/2 teaspoon cayenne pepper
- 1/2 salt
- 1/ 2 teaspoon black pepper

Preparation Instructions

1. Combine ingredients in a bowl. Marinate steaks at least 2 hours.

Yield: about 2 cups

Chapter Twelve

Right to Work:
A Broad Interpretation

Livingston v. Dobbs, 559 So. 2d 569 (Ala. 1990)

Euell Dobbs and William Livingston opened a restaurant in Dothan, Alabama, called Dobbs Famous Bar-B-Que. Shortly thereafter, both men married, and the respective Mrs. Dobbs and Mrs. Livingston worked for years in their husbands' business as *unpaid* waitresses until they finally took retirement. Eventually, Dobbs purchased Livingston's partnership interest in the business, and the contract of sale contained the following non-competition clause:

> The seller and his wife, **who is a signatory to this agreement for the sole purpose of this provision** and who by the execution hereof acknowledges the sufficiency of the consideration for the agreements herein contained, agree that neither will directly or indirectly, as an individual partner, officer, director or shareholder in any corporation, or employee or agent of either, operate or participate in the operation of any business in competition with Dobbs Bar-B-Que or its successor, in any

> area within a 100 mile radius of Dothan, Alabama, for a period of ten (10) years. (emphasis added)

Shortly after the sale of Dobbs Barbeque, the Livingstons divorced. In the divorce settlement, Marie Livingston was awarded the unpaid balance of the purchase price of the business.

A few years later, Marie became involved in the start of another barbecue restaurant in Dothan, known as Old South Barbeque. She loaned money to Old South's founder, and she agreed to work in the fledgling restaurant as its manager. In her efforts to get the new business started, Livingston hired some of the employees from Dobbs Barbeque. Dobbs subsequently brought this action to enjoin Marie from participating in the operation of Old South Barbeque.

Marie contended that the noncompetition clause should not be enforced because it did not fall within one of the exceptions in the statute. The statute rendered the noncompetition agreements generally invalid but provided certain exceptions to those who (a) sell a business, or (b) are employed by the business being sold. Marie claimed that she did not fall within either exception, and therefore, the contract provision restraining her employment was *void.* Marie explained, first of all, that she was not the seller of the partnership interest because her husband was the sole owner at the time of the sale, and secondly, that she was not employed in the business because she received no compensation for her work as a waitress. The court found her arguments persuasive.

As the court initially noted, contracts restraining employment have been traditionally disfavored. With that in mind, the court turned to the language of the contract itself and compared it with the exceptions outlined in the statute. The contract provided that "the seller and his wife" covenant not to compete, but the contract went on to identify William solely as the "seller." Marie was mentioned nowhere in the contract other than in the noncompetition clause. The noncompetition clause itself confirmed that she was not the seller, because it explicitly contained the phrase "the seller and his wife, who is a signatory to this agreement for the sole purpose of this provision."

It was clear from this language that the noncompetition clause purported to forbid Marie from engaging in a competing business, but unless she fell within one of the exceptions set out in the statute, the clause was void and of no effect. Clearly, the court concluded, Marie did not fall into the exception of "one who sells the goodwill of a business."

Dobbs persisted, arguing that Marie should in fact be considered one of the sellers because she was receiving the balance of the purchase price owed by him to the seller. The court was not sympathetic to that argument, either, because ownership was determined at the time of the sale, and Marie was not an owner at that time. The record was clear that Marie received the balance due on the purchase price *after* the sale as part of her divorce settlement.

Furthermore, it was also obvious to the court that Marie also did not fit within the exception provided for one "employed as an agent, servant or employee." Livingston was not "employed," as that term is commonly used, and she received no compensation from Dobbs Bar-B-Que as an agent, servant, or employee.

The court made it clear, however, that it was not holding that in all cases nonowner spouses were free to disregard covenants that were binding on their marital partners. A person may be enjoined from operating a competing business if he or she receives assistance in operating the business from the one bound by the covenant. But there was simply no evidence of such assistance in this case.

The moral of the court's ruling was clear: the next time you buy a barbecue business, it's important to first make sure that the owner's wife was a *paid* employee.

Cue Spot 12

Unforgettable Garlic-Basil Chicken Marinade

Ingredients

- 1/2 cup olive oil
- 1/4 cup red wine vinegar
- 1 clove garlic, chopped
- 1 tablespoon basil leaves
- 1 tablespoon red onion, finely chopped
- 2 teaspoons salt
- 1 teaspoon black pepper

Preparation Instructions

1. Stir ingredients together in a bowl.
2. Transfer marinade to a gallon-sized sealable plastic bag, and add chicken.
3. Refrigerate for at least 3 hours, preferably longer.

Yield: about 1 cup

Chapter Thirteen

Sauce Maker: Litigating the Insurance Contract

Holsum Foods v. Home Insurance Co., 469 N.W.2d 918 (Wisc. 1991)

Holsum Foods is in the business of preparing and packaging foods, and it entered into a contract with Kingsford Products to produce the ever-popular K.C. Masterpiece Barbecue Sauce. Kingsford purchased the majority of basic ingredients and materials (including the jar, label, and cap) from separate vendors. It then shipped the materials to Holsum's processing plant in Waukesha, Wisconsin. Holsum mixed Kingsford's ingredients with a sweetener, cooked the mixture, and packaged it into jars. The product was then shipped at Kingsford's direction.

At some point in the process, it was discovered that the bottling operation was chipping jars and depositing small glass chips in the sauce. Holsum and Kingsford agreed to suspend production, and all of the barbecue sauce was stored pending an investigation. Sampling indicated that approximately 2 to 3 percent of the bottles contained glass. However, it was agreed that none of the finished product could be released to the public because there was no way of determining which ones were contaminated. Holsum agreed to pay Kingsford $1.3 million over three years.

Holsum then made a claim against its liability insurance carrier, Home Insurance Company. Home refused coverage, citing exclusion (n), which specifically denied coverage "to property damage to the named insured's products arising out of such products." The purpose of the exclusion, a standard exclusion used by the industry, was to prevent the insured from using its products liability coverage as a form of property insurance to cover the cost of repairing or replacing its own defectively manufactured products.

This "injury to products" exclusion was intended to exclude insurance for damage *to* the product by the named insured, not for damage caused *by* the insured's product. Thus, exclusion (n) excluded coverage for the risk that the insured's manufactured product might not turn out as it was planned.

Home asserted that the barbecue sauce was Holsum's product and that the company was attempting to use the coverage to recover the cost of having produced a defect in the product. Holsum claimed, on the other hand, that the sauce was actually Kingsford's product, not Holsum's, and that Holsum's actions caused damage to Kingsford's product.

According to the court, the dispositive issue was whether Holsum was in the business of *manufacturing* a product, as opposed to providing services, when it mixed, cooked, jarred, and packaged ingredients provided by a customer. The court held that Holsum was indeed making a product, and therefore, was not covered by the liability policy because it specifically excluded property damage "to the named insured's products."

The court began its analysis with the policy definition of a product. The term "named insured's products" in the exclusion was defined as "goods or products manufactured, sold, handled or distributed by the named insured, including any container thereof."

The court analyzed this policy definition using the typical maxims. Words should be given their common, everyday meaning, and when the terms are plain and unambiguous, the court will construe the contract as it stands. The court explained that the plain meaning of the word *manufacture* was "something made from raw materials by hand or by machinery," and thus, Holsum was manufacturing a product.

Holsum was not about to give up. It then argued that even if the court held it to have manufactured a product, the property damage claim did not "arise out of such products" as required by the exclusion. Holsum asserted that the completed product did not cause any harm, but rather, the harm was caused by the manufacturing process to the ingredients supplied by Kingsford. In other words, the so-called occurrence took place before the product even existed.

The court, alas, did not buy that argument either, noting that as used in a liability insurance policy, the words "arising out of" were very broad, and were commonly understood to mean "originating from." Thus, it was only necessary that there be some causal relationship between the injury and the risk for which coverage was provided. In the court's view, the harm grew out of the manufacturing process while making the product, and the property damage was indeed *to* the products.

Finally, Holsum offered yet another argument, this one again focusing on the words "arising out of." It pointed out that only 2 to 3 percent of the jars were damaged, and that 97 percent were free from defect. Therefore, the defect-free jars were not "property damage arising out of such products."

The court was, once again, not convinced. Home's exclusion, the court concluded, unambiguously applied to *all* of the insured's products if the property damage arose out of all "or any part of such products."

In spite of all its efforts to the contrary, Holsum found itself stuck with over a million dollars worth of barbecue sauce that was perfectly fine—if you don't mind yours mixed with a little glass.

Cue Spot 13

Incredible Pork Tenderloin Mop Sauce

Ingredients

- 4 pork tenderloins

For Rub

- 2 teaspoons brown sugar
- 1 teaspoon paprika
- 1 teaspoon chili powder
- 1 teaspoon cumin
- 1 teaspoon salt
- 1/4 teaspoon cayenne pepper
- 1/4 teaspoon black pepper

For Sauce

- 1/3 cup ketchup
- 1/4 cup cider vinegar
- 2 teaspoons molasses
- 2 teaspoons Worcestershire sauce

Preparation Instructions

1. For spice rub, mix rub ingredients in a bowl. Apply mixture over pork and let stand 15 minutes before grilling.

Cue Spot 13 (continued)

2. Meanwhile, combine ingredients for the mop sauce mix, and drench pork during the cooking process, according to taste.

Yield: 4 servings

Chapter Fourteen

The BBQ Stand: Limiting the Ordinance

Fincher v. City of Union, 196 S.E. 1 (S.C. 1938)

Arthur Fincher purchased a small parcel of land in the downtown area of Union, South Carolina, on which was standing a dilapidated tin-and-wood building. It was generally known around the community the purpose for which Fincher was buying the property. He removed the old structure and erected in its place a handsome brick-and-glass building, and he complied with all the license laws and all other regulations of the city. Then he opened up Fincher's Barbecue for business.

A substantial portion of Fincher's trade was done after eleven at night, and he kept his restaurant open until two or three in the morning. Operating a barbecue stand, the court observed, is a lawful and legitimate business, noting that a particular business may of course become a nuisance if not maintained in a decent, respectable, and peaceful manner.

But it was never claimed that Fincher or any of his employees were guilty of disorderly behavior. Rather, some of the patrons from time to time were engaged in boisterous conduct, loud talking, and laughing, frequently accompanied by profane and obscene language which emanated from automobiles parked near the barbecue stand. It appeared the only residents who were disturbed by these patrons were those who lived immediately adjacent to the restaurant. Other nearby residents testified that Fincher's business was conducted in an orderly manner, and that they had not been disturbed by Fincher, his employees, or his patrons.

In response to the vociferous complaints of the few neighbors, the city council passed the following ordinance, which was clearly aimed at Fincher's Barbecue:

> That on and after the passage of this ordinance it shall be unlawful for any person owning, operating or employed at a barbecue stand, located in any residential area of the City of Union, to allow the same to remain open between the hours of 11:00 o'clock P.M., and 6:00 o'clock A.M., except on Saturdays, when they may remain open until 12:00 o'clock midnight.
>
> Most importantly, the ordinance then defined the term "residential area":
>
> The word "Residential Area" used herein shall include any section of the City of Union where two or more houses, used for residential purposes, are located on abutting property.

Regardless of the numerous businesses in the vicinity of Fincher's barbecue stand, the ordinance classified it being located within a "residential area" of the city. Undaunted, Fincher brought suit questioning the constitutionality of the ordinance, and the trial judge was receptive to this argument, finding the ordinance to be unreasonable in that (a) it sought to interfere with a legitimate business without just cause and in violation of the U.S. and state constitutions, and (b) it attempted to hold the business owner responsible for certain incidents of disorderly conduct by those not connected with his business, and over whom he had no control.

The judge further found that Fincher had been deprived of his property rights because the ordinance discriminated between him and others in a similar line of business.

The court approached the case with a sympathetic ear toward those who resided adjacent to the barbecue lot. However, the court explained that the encroachment of business into a residential section of a city typically enhances property values, even as it diminishes its suitableness for residential purposes. The court reasoned that if a few residents could continue to reside in a business area, and a city ordinance could declare such area "residential" notwithstanding the fact that businesses greatly exceeded homes, the expansion of commercial areas would come to a screeching halt.

The court also held that Fincher was deprived of a substantial use of his property, not by reason of his conduct, but that of others. The court assumed that the city had general ordinances against loud and boisterous conduct, the use of profanity, and disorderly conduct. It was, the court observed, the duty of the police to preserve peace and good order in a business section. Certainly the remaining residents in a business district had the right to expect those laws to be enforced, which would remedy most of the evils sought to be corrected by the present ordinance.

In the end, Mr. Fincher would be allowed to keep his barbecue stand, but his rowdy patrons might have to pipe down just a bit.

Cue Spot 14

Not-Your-Ordinary BBQ Beans

Ingredients

- 1 pound pinto beans (soaked overnight)
- 3/4 pound ground chuck
- 7 cups water
- 1 onion, diced
- 1 clove garlic, minced
- 1 teaspoon paprika
- 1 teaspoon thyme
- 1 tablespoon chili powder
- 3/4 cup ketchup
- 1/4 cup brown sugar
- 1/3 cup mustard
- 2 tablespoons Worcestershire sauce
- 1/4 teaspoon salt
- 1/4 teaspoon black pepper

Preparation Instructions

1. Place beans in a large pot of water and bring to a boil. Reduce heat to a steady boil and cook until tender.
2. In a saucepan, sauté onion and garlic.

3. Add ground chuck and cook, stirring often, until meat is brown. Stir in remaining ingredients.
4. Pour ingredients into a pot with the beans and stir well.

Yield: 4 servings

Part III

Name Game

Chapter Fifteen

Sauce Wars:
Enforcing the Mark

Kraft General Foods v. Allied Old English, 831 F. Supp. 123 (S.D.N.Y. 1993)

Kraft General Foods manufactures the very popular line of Bull's-Eye barbecue sauce, and sales eventually became significant, rising to almost 45 million dollars a year. Bull's-Eye was marketed extensively in print advertisements and television commercials, and Kraft spent about five million dollars a year promoting the product.

Since its introduction, Bull's-Eye was sold in a clear glass bottle with a dark-brown label featuring a bull's head at the top center of the logo, with the trade name *Bull's-Eye* in white below that, and the words *Big Bold Taste* on a colored banner at the bottom center of the logo. Kraft had obtained trademark registrations for the mark Bull's Eye and the bull's head design.

The Allied Old English company began to produce and test market a barbecue sauce under the similar name of Raging Bull. Allied applied for trademark registration of its mark, and no opposition was filed. Although Allied knew that Kraft's sauce was on the market, no one at the company seemed concerned about trademark infringement. The Raging Bull packaging included a sketch of "an angry, excited bull." The label was black, and dark red was chosen for the bull's head to play up the "raging" aspect.

In its petition for false designation of origin, trademark and trade dress infringement, unfair competition, and dilution, Kraft alleged that Raging Bull infringed upon the trademark rights of the Bull's-Eye name and packaging. Kraft argued that the defendant's use of the Raging Bull name and the packaging used in conjunction with it were likely to cause confusion among the purchasers. Accordingly, Kraft claimed that it was continuously and irreparably harmed while the product stayed on the market in its present marketing form.

To determine whether there was a "likelihood of confusion," the court considered the following factors: (1) the strength of the prior owner's mark, (2) the similarity between the two marks, (3) the competitive proximity of the products, (4) actual confusion, (5) the defendant's good faith, and (6) the sophistication of the buyers.

Strength of the Mark. The court found that the Bull's-Eye was a strong mark for two reasons. First, the mark was conceptually distinct. Second, the mark had acquired strong secondary meaning in the minds of the public. Thus, the mark came to identify not only the goods but also their source, even though the consuming public might not know the actual name of the producer. Kraft had established secondary meaning in its mark through years of exclusive use, extensive advertising, commercial success, and unsolicited media coverage.

The Similarity of the Marks. The court found that Kraft sustained its burden of demonstrating that the Raging Bull mark was confusingly similar to the Bull's-Eye mark. The similarity of the bull's head designs and the closeness of the product names clearly created products that were confusingly similar.

Proximity of the Products. In this case, the products were obviously in direct competition with each other.

Evidence of Actual Confusion. Kraft presented to the court a market survey suggesting that a significant number of consumers were likely to confuse the products when making purchasing decisions. The court accepted this as credible evidence of confusion.

Good Faith. The court found that there was some evidence that Allied selected the Raging Bull mark to capitalize on the favorable image and goodwill that the Bull's-Eye mark had developed in the minds of consumers. Allied was aware that Bull's-Eye was a leading barbecue sauce and would be Raging Bull's principal competition in the marketplace. Allied simply did not take the care necessary to ensure that its mark did not infringe and usurp the goodwill of the prior mark.

Sophistication of the Buyers. The products sold by both plaintiff and defendant were relatively low-priced items intermingled with numerous other barbecue sauces on supermarket shelves. Consumers were likely to purchase these items without devoting much time and attention to the decision. The purchase of either party's product was not a major expenditure for most consumers, and the packaging was unlikely to be carefully scrutinized before making a purchase. Under such circumstances, the likelihood that consumers would assume that Allied's product originated with a source that had some connection to Kraft was substantially increased.

Having carefully considered and weighed these factors, the court found that Kraft had demonstrated that there was in fact sufficient evidence of likelihood of confusion to warrant the issuance of a preliminary injunction.

Alas, the Raging Bull would rage no more.

Cue Spot 15

Heavenly Potato Salad

Ingredients

- 4 medium potatoes, cooked and diced
- 1 cup mayonnaise
- 1 tablespoon cider vinegar
- 1 tablespoon sugar
- 1/2 tablespoon mustard
- 1/2 teaspoon salt
- 1/2 teaspoon garlic powder
- 1/2 teaspoon black pepper
- 2 celery stalks, diced
- 1 cup onion, minced
- 3 hard-boiled eggs, chopped
- 1/ 2 teaspoon paprika

Preparation Instructions

1. Boil peeled potatoes until done. Cool to room temperature, and chop into small chunks.
2. Combine other ingredients in another bowl, and mix with potatoes.

Yield: 4 servings

BBQ

Chapter Sixteen

Barbecue Joints:
Drawing the Line

Barbecue Marx, Inc. v. 551 Ogden, Inc., 235 F.3d 1041 (7th Cir. 2000)

Interestingly enough, even the seemingly casual world of neighborhood barbecue joints is not without some intense competition. The owner of the very popular Chicago destination called Smoke Daddy aggressively moved to protect its turf by bringing a trademark infringement action against the competition, who planned to use the name Bone Daddy for its forthcoming restaurant.

The trial court granted the preliminary injunction, finding that the marks were confusingly similar in appearance and suggestion. The court largely based its finding on the tonal similarities of the words *smoke* and *bone*. Both words, the court noted, had a long *o* and were only one syllable long. Furthermore, the court found that both marks evoked images of "slow cooked, smoked barbecue, usually ribs on the bone." Bone Daddy appealed the ruling.

By way of background, Smoke Daddy is located on the Near West Side of Chicago and features live music, mostly blues. It is a small, 1,500-square-foot diner that seats about forty people, and its logo features the words *Smoke Daddy* sitting atop a pair of wings and smoke. Not only is it a successful restaurant, but food critics have recognized it as one of the best barbecue venues in Chicago.

The owners of another critically acclaimed restaurant, the Twisted Spoke, decided to enter the barbecue business. Looking for a name, they were allegedly inspired by the movie *The Nightmare Before Christmas*, in which one character asks a skeleton, "What's up, bone daddy?" However, as it turned out, they were also quite aware of Smoke Daddy and had dined there several times.

Bone Daddy was located only a few blocks from the Twisted Spoke and about a mile and a half from Smoke Daddy. The sizeable 5,000-square-foot restaurant was a little different from its predecessor; it featured a bar and two dining rooms that were decorated in a modern style. Bone Daddy planned to feature live entertainment, including bluegrass and acoustic, but not blues. The Bone Daddy logo featured a pig dressed like a gangster, smoking a cigar and the words *Bone Daddy*.

In this case, the defendant readily accepted that Smoke Daddy was a protectable trademark. However, it argued that the preliminary injunction was granted in error because the plaintiff did not meet its burden of proof with regard to the likelihood of confusion. Seven factors comprise the likelihood of confusion test: (1) similarity between the marks in appearance and suggestion, (2) similarity of the products, (3) area and manner of concurrent use, (4) degree of care likely to be exercised by consumers, (5) strength of the mark, (6) actual confusion, and (7) intent of the defendant to "palm off" his product as that of another. The likelihood of confusion test is an equitable balancing test. No single factor is dispositive, and courts may assign varying weights to each of the factors in different cases.

Similarity in Appearance and Suggestion. The trial court focused most heavily on the first factor, finding that the marks were confusingly similar in appearance and suggestion. The appellate court agreed that the words sounded alike and evoked similar imagery.

However, Smoke Daddy's rectangular mark depicted the words *Smoke Daddy* on top of a pair of wings and smoke, while Bone Daddy's mark prominently displayed a pig clad like a gangster and the words *Bone Daddy*. The marks, in the appellate court's mind, were visually distinct. Because the public would encounter the marks in written and spoken form, the court believed it was essential to consider the marks' visual characteristics. The court concluded that the visual appearance significantly undercut the strength of the plaintiff's argument that the marks were similar.

Similarity of Products. The second factor is the similarity of the products. The trial court noted that both restaurants served (or planned to serve) the same product: barbecue. However, the restaurants' ambiances and themes were vastly different. Smoke Daddy was a small restaurant, seated only about forty people, was decorated in a 1950s style, and focused heavily on blues music. In contrast, Bone Daddy was a much larger restaurant that styled itself as "irreverent," and its interior and food were quite than different from its competition. The appellate court did not find clear error, but it certainly weakened the trial court's finding in favor of the plaintiff.

Area and Manner of Concurrent Use. The trial court emphasized that the restaurants were located in the same neighborhood because they were a mile and a half apart. But the appellate court noted that Smoke Daddy was located in Wicker Park and Bone Daddy was situated in River West. These neighborhoods are in the heart of Chicago, and in such a densely populated area that a mile and a half is quite a distance, especially in an area filled with dozens of restaurants. The appellate court found that the district court committed clear error when it weighed this factor in favor of Smoke Daddy.

Degree of Care Likely to be Exercised by Consumers. The trial court also weighed the fourth factor in favor of Smoke Daddy. The appellate court believed this too was clear error. The trial court based its finding on the idea that "although a careful patron might look up the address, write it down, and follow directions, some others might hop in the cab or car and wing it—perhaps to the wrong restaurant."

There was little convincing evidence on the record to support this conclusion. Smoke Daddy argued that many people do not consider a $20 dinner expensive and might forget the precise name of a restaurant recommended to them. The appellate court did not find this argument persuasive because most of Smoke Daddy's customers were "barbecue aficionados," and such customers can be expected to exercise a reasonable degree of care when planning to dine at a restaurant of Smoke Daddy's caliber.

Strength of the Mark. The trial court did not address the strength of Smoke Daddy's mark. The appellate court believed, however, that this factor should be weighed in favor of the plaintiff, which had been in existence for six years and had built a reputation for good barbecue.

Actual Confusion. The sixth factor is actual confusion. Because Bone Daddy had not yet opened its doors, it would be exceedingly difficult for Smoke Daddy to find evidence of actual confusion. However, in the mind of the appellate court, this difficulty did not excuse Smoke Daddy from providing *some* evidence. The company could have conducted a survey of potential consumers to compare the two restaurants or could have solicited testimony from an expert in marketing or psychology. The appellate court concluded that the trial court committed clear error when it weighed this factor in favor of Smoke Daddy.

Intent to "Palm Off" the Product as that of Another. The last factor is the intent of the defendant to "palm off" the product as that of another. Bone Daddy admitted that its owners had previously eaten at Smoke Daddy and discussed the similarity of the two names. However, this knowledge alone was not enough to show intent. It was relevant to note that Bone Daddy's location was closer to the Twisted Spoke than it was to Smoke Daddy, neutralizing an inference of bad intent that could be derived from the proximity of the two restaurants. Given the evidence presented, the court concluded that this factor supported Bone Daddy.

Balancing the Factors. After considering each of the factors, the appellate court concluded that there was not enough evidence to support a preliminary injunction. The key factors in this case were the lack of evidence regarding Bone Daddy's malicious intent and the relative absence of actual confusion on the part of consumers. These factors strongly militated against imposing a preliminary injunction, and the Seventh Circuit Court of Appeals therefore reversed the trial court's judgment.

As a result, the stakes in the Chicago barbecue world were notched up a bit, and Smoke Daddy would soon have to contend with brisk(et) competition from Bone Daddy.

Cue Spot 16

Over-the-Top Cole Slaw

Ingredients

- 1 head cabbage, finely shredded
- 2 carrots, finely chopped
- 2 tablespoons onion, finely chopped
- 1/2 cup mayonnaise
- 1/3 cup white sugar
- 2 tablespoons lemon juice
- 2 tablespoons white vinegar
- 1/2 teaspoon salt
- 1/8 teaspoon black pepper

Preparation Instructions

1. Mix cabbage, carrots, and onion in a large salad bowl.
2. Stir together other ingredients in a separate bowl until smooth.
3. Pour dressing over cabbage mixture and mix thoroughly.
4. Cover bowl and refrigerate at least 2 hours.

Yield: 4 servings

Chapter Seventeen

Charcoal Briquettes:

Extending the Dynasty

Kingsford Products Co. v. Kingsfords, Inc., 715 F. Supp. 1013 (D. Kan. 1989)

Almost anyone who has ever set match to grill has heard of Kingsford charcoal. In the world of briquettes, it is a truly ubiquitous brand, and the name The Kingsford Products Company appears prominently on the outside of its bags. The company also sells wood chips and lighter fluid, and it later acquired the popular K.C. Masterpiece line of barbecue sauce.

On the other hand, the similarly named Kingsfords, Inc. was a small company that sold barbecue sauce under the name Original K Barbecue Sauce. The company was owned by Stephen and Marianne Kingsford (that *really* was their name) of DeSoto, Kansas. The label on their barbecue sauce conspicuously bore the name of Kingsford, Inc.

The Kingsford charcoal people promptly brought suit against the Kingsford barbecue sauce people, seeking to enjoin the defendants from using the Kingsford name in any way, boldly and unabashedly contending that its trademark extended to barbecue sauce and even to barbecuing in general. The plaintiff further asserted that the defendant's use of the Kingsford mark created consumer confusion regarding the source of the defendant's product. The defendant countered with the argument that barbecue sauce was not even a product marketed by the plaintiff at the time the defendant began selling its line of sauce. The defendant further argued that the plaintiff, in any event, had not shown a secondary meaning of the surname Kingsford in barbecue sauce, and thus, was not entitled to trademark protection.

Likelihood of Consumer Confusion. After reviewing the evidence presented at trial, the court found that the plaintiff had not presented sufficient evidence to indicate its most important contention—confusion among consumers. The plaintiff's manager of consumer information, Sandy Sullivan, even admitted that the company received only *two* inquiries regarding the defendant's Original K Barbecue Sauce in a two-year time period. Additionally, the deposition testimony of a number of grocery store checkers stated that they never received *any* inquiries from consumers indicating confusion regarding the source of the defendant's sauce.

Related Products Doctrine. Additionally, the plaintiff argued that it was entitled to trademark protection on barbecue sauce products under the related products doctrine, contending that the defendants' barbecue sauce product was sufficiently related to the plaintiff's charcoal and wood chip products to entitle it to trademark protection in barbecue sauce. The court disagreed.

Future plans. The court found that the plaintiff was not entitled to trademark protection merely because it hoped to someday market a barbecue sauce prominently bearing the Kingsford name.

Secondary Meaning. The court also found that the plaintiff had failed to show that the Kingsford mark had a secondary meaning regarding barbecue sauce, or barbecuing in general. The plaintiff's use of the mark on the K.C. Masterpiece Barbecue Sauce was not prominent, and its use did not create an identity of Kingsford with barbecue sauce. The plaintiff simply used the Kingsford house mark on this product, indicating it was the manufacturer of the product. Moreover, and perhaps most importantly, this use of the mark did not occur until *after* the defendants were marketing their own barbecue sauce.

The court recognized that Kingsford had great name recognition regarding charcoal briquettes but that the plaintiff had failed to bridge the gap between charcoal and barbecue sauce to create a secondary meaning in the name for barbecue sauce.

Good Faith. According to the court, the individual defendants acted in good faith in using their own surname on Original K Barbecue Sauce. The defendants had pride in their family name, which had been associated with another successful food product (Kingsford Cornstarch) in the past. The court found that the defendant's actions revealed no bad faith or intent to trade on the plaintiff's trademark.

By judicial fiat, then, the Kingsfords of DeSoto, Kansas, who most certainly did a little dance every time they thought how lucky they were to have such a name, could now sell their barbecue sauce with total impunity.

Cue Spot 17

Incomparable Sourdough Biscuits

Ingredients

- 1 cup flour
- 1/4 teaspoon salt
- 1/2 teaspoon baking soda
- 2 teaspoons baking powder
- 1/3 cup margarine
- 1 cup sourdough starter

Preparation Instructions

1. Mix ingredients together.
2. Place dough onto a floured board and knead briefly. Roll dough to 3/4 inch, and cut out biscuits. Place the biscuits on an ungreased baking sheet.
3. Bake at 425°F for about 15 minutes until slightly brown.

Yield: 8 biscuits

BBQ &
SUSHI

Chapter Eighteen

Marketing Madness:
A Matter of Labeling

Hesmer Foods, Inc. v. Campbell Soup Company, 346 F.2d 356 (7th Cir. 1965)

Hesmer Foods decided to tangle with the big boys. Most of Hesmer's distribution was within a hundred mile radius of Evansville, Indiana, but its most popular product, Beanee Barbecue, was sold nationwide.

Hesmer had secured a federal trademark on a product known as Beanee Barbecue, whose major ingredients were beans, water, catsup, and pork. Hesmer was proud of the fact that 8.4 percent of its product was hickory-smoked, pit-barbecue pork. The remaining 91.6 percent was not subject to open-fire cooking, though the beans were cooked in an open vessel.

Campbell Soup Company began marketing a canned product known as Barbecue Beans, which contained three kinds of beans but no meat. This product customarily sold for half the price of Beanee Barbecue, and it was marketed under its ubiquitous label with the name *Campbell* in white script on a red background.

Hesmer sought an injunction as a result of Campbell's alleged trademark infringement and unfair competition by labeling one of its products in a way alleged to be both (a) false and misleading, and (b) confusingly similar to the way in which Hesmer labeled Beanee Barbecue.

At the conclusion of the plaintiff's case, the trial court sustained the defendant's motion for a directed verdict. The evidence showed that there were a large number of products on the market called barbecue beans. All of them were meatless or essentially meatless, and some of them were on the market before the introduction of the plaintiff's product.

On appeal, the plaintiff complained that when Campbell put its barbecued beans on the market selling at a much-reduced price, the sale of its Beanee Barbecue was adversely affected. The plaintiff's allegation regarding the Campbell label was its inclusion of the words "Fresh-off-the-open-fire flavor, with the zip and tang of picnic dinners cooked over glowing embers." The plaintiff pointed out that Campbell's product was not cooked in an open vessel, over an open fire, or over glowing embers. Hesmer also complained that Campbell's label included the picture of an open kettle full of beans and that it claimed ingredients that its product did not contain but that Hesmer's product did.

The plaintiff cited previous judicial decisions to the effect that the critical test was "likelihood of confusion," and it claimed that in the instant case, it had made a *prima facie* showing of such confusion. But unfortunately for Hesmer, there was no proof that Campbell was selling its barbecue beans as the plaintiff's product. In fact, the plaintiff's president admitted on the witness stand that he knew of no one who had purchased Campbell's product thinking it was Hesmer's product and that the labels were so dissimilar in appearance that only "a person that was without vision could be confused."

The appellate court hit the nail on the head with this poignant observation: "Some of the difficulty in this case arises from the fact that the word 'barbecue' can be used as a noun, as a verb, or as an adjective." Campbell's use of the words *barbecue beans* is not a trademark, the court remarked, but rather a description of its product—that is, beans that were suitable for use at a barbecue. The court went on to note that it was obvious the granting of the trademark Beanee Barbecue did not convey to the plaintiff a monopoly for preparing beans for all barbecues.

The plaintiff then argued that the use of the word *barbecue*, which appeared on the defendant's label between the words *Campbell's* and *beans*, necessarily implied that the product contained meat. The plaintiff conceded that Campbell could properly name its product "Campbell's Beans in Barbecue Sauce." Thus, the plaintiffs claimed that the word *barbecue*, when used as an adjective with the word *beans*, implicated a meat product. The court saw no basis for such an argument. On every label of the defendant's Barbecue Beans was a statement of the contents of the can that appeared in readable print, and there was no mention of any meat. The label also clearly contained the following statement of content: "3 Kinds Of Beans In Mild Barbecue Sauce."

In the end, the court concluded that the plaintiff was required to show some likelihood of competitive injury arising from a false representation made by Campbell in marketing its product and that it had failed to do so.

The Beanee Barbecue people, now completely stripped of their case, were on their own in the rough-and-tumble world of *meatless* barbecue beans.

Cue Spot 18

Outrageous Apricot Fried Pies

Ingredients

- Cooking oil (for frying)
- 2 tablespoons cinnamon sugar

Apricot filling

- 2 cups dried apricots, diced
- 1 jar of apricot jam (8 ounces)
- 6 ounces apricot nectar
- 1 cup sugar

Crust

- 3 cups flour
- 1 tablespoon powdered sugar
- 1/2 teaspoon salt
- 1 tablespoon white vinegar
- 1 egg yolk
- 1 stick butter
- 3/4 cup water

Preparation Instructions

Filling

1. Combine apricot filling ingredients in a medium saucepan and simmer over medium heat, stirring frequently, for 10 to 15 minutes.

Crust

1. Mix crust ingredients in bowl.
2. Refrigerate dough ball for about 30 minutes.

Final Assembly

1. On a floured board, roll out dough to 1/8-inch or less thickness. Cut or stamp dough into 6-inch round circles
2. Spoon about 2 tablespoons of filling into center of each circle of dough. Fold in half and press the edges together with a fork. Poke the top of the crust with the fork.
3. Pour several inches of cooking oil into a large, deep, heavy-bottomed pan or Dutch oven.
4. Carefully add pie pockets to the hot oil in batches and deep fry until golden brown. Sprinkle with cinnamon sugar.

Yield: about 12 pies

Part IV

The Ultimate Dilemma

Chapter Nineteen

Anything for Good Cue:

Even a Job

Haney v. City of Los Angeles, 109 Cal. App. 4th 1 (2003)

A Los Angeles Police Department employment board found Officer Bryan Haney guilty of leaving his post without authorization and submitting a daily field report that he knew contained false information. A majority of the three-person board recommended that Haney be removed from his position. The chief of police accepted the recommendation and terminated his employment. Haney petitioned for administrative review, contending that the charges leveled against him (a) were barred by the statute of limitations, or (b) constituted an abuse of administrative discretion.

On the Memorial Day in question, Haney and Officers Stephen Morris, Perry Alvarez, and Toni Di Paolo decided to celebrate the holiday with a little barbecue. Alvarez and Di Paolo obtained permission from security guard Ocampo to dine on a portion of the naval base in San Pedro, California, that contained abandoned naval housing. They then obtained a grill from Haney and drove to the naval base, arriving there about noon. Ocampo admitted them through a locked gate.

Alvarez and Di Paolo lit the grill and prepared the food. Haney and Morris arrived about thirty minutes later. The four officers ate and left the base about 2:00 P.M., leaving behind the grill, which was too hot to put in the patrol car.

All four officers had been assigned to foot patrol at morning roll call. Alvarez and Di Paolo submitted a false field report, which stated that they monitored the San Pedro bicycle race from 11:00 A.M. until 2:00 P.M. Haney and Morris also submitted a false field report, which stated that they were engaged in foot patrol activities from 11:00 A.M. to 12:30 P.M. and from 1:30 to 1:45 P.M. and that they took a lunch break from 4:30 to 5:15 P.M.

Sergeant William Forman, who was the LAPD liaison to those in charge of the naval base, heard of the barbecue and inquired further. Sergeant Forman asked Officer Cirilo to determine whether the officers involved were affiliated with the LAPD. At that point, Sergeant Forman was concerned only that an event had taken place without his consent. While this would be a breach of protocol, he had no reason to suspect anything further. There was a question about the time frame of the barbecue, but due to conflicting schedules and his involvement in training, he did not have a chance to personally speak with the officers.

Sergeant Forman completed a routine attendance audit, and at this point, he became concerned that this incidence of misconduct might be indicative of a broader problem. The fact that Alvarez and Di Paolo were two of the officers involved in the barbecue incident heightened his suspicions that there might be misconduct. A preliminary investigation was ordered, and it recommended that charges be filed against the officers for abandonment of their duty posts without authorization and for submitting false field reports.

When confronted, Haney admitted that he abandoned his post without permission and that his field report contained inaccurate information. Haney characterized his misconduct as nothing more than an isolated event that did not harm the public service.

The court saw matters a little differently. In its view, Haney and his fellow officers planned the meal, purchased food, and attended the barbecue, performing all of these acts when they should have been attending their foot patrol assignments. Haney and the others then knowingly falsified an official LAPD document to conceal the time spent at the barbecue and their abandonment of duty.

The court concluded that these acts indisputably caused harm to the public service. Haney deprived the public of police protection by his absence from patrol duties, and he demonstrated both disloyalty to the LAPD and a serious lack of integrity. The court observed that police officer integrity is vital to effective law enforcement and that public trust in the department and its officers did not exist otherwise.

All in all, it was a very expensive day for Officer Haney. Let's just put it this way: anyone who will risk his job for brisket has a very serious barbecue monkey on his back.

Cue Spot 19

Stupendous Cherry Cobbler

Ingredients

- 1/2 cup butter
- 1 cup flour
- 1 cup sugar
- 1 teaspoon baking powder
- 1 cup milk
- 2 cups pitted sour cherries
- 3/4 cup sugar
- 1 tablespoon flour

Preparation Instructions

1. Preheat the oven to 350°F. Place butter in a 9x13-inch baking dish, and melt while the oven is preheating. Remove from the stove after the butter has melted.
2. In a medium bowl, stir together 1 cup of flour, 1 cup of sugar, baking powder, and milk until well blended. Pour batter into the pan over the butter.
3. Place cherries into a bowl and toss with the remaining 3/4 cup of sugar and 1 tablespoon of flour. Distribute cherry mixture evenly over batter.
4. Bake for about an hour until golden brown.

Yield: about 12 slices

Index

About the Author

Cecil C. Kuhne III is a litigator in the Dallas office of Fulbright & Jaworski L.L.P. In his search for the perfect barbecue joint, he has consumed much more "Q" than he cares to admit, and his favorite bumper sticker sums it up well: "So much BBQ, so little time."